100 Facts About
Sharks

100 Facts About
Sharks

David O'Doherty
Claudia O'Doherty
& Mike Ahern

SQUARE PEG

◙ SQUARE PEG

Published by Square Peg
2 4 6 8 10 9 7 5 3 1

First published in Great Britatin and Ireland in 2011 by Square Peg
Random House, 20 Vauxhall Bridge Road, London SW1V 2SA

www.rbooks.co.uk

Addresses for companies within The Random House Group Limited can be found at:
www.randomhouse.co.uk/offices.htm

The Random House Group Limited Reg. No. 954009

A CIP catalogue record for this book is available from the British Library

ISBN 9780224086769

The Random House Group Limited makes every effort to ensure that the papers used in its books are made from trees that have
been legally sourced from well-managed and credibly certified forests. Our paper procurement policy can be found at:
www.randomhouse.co.uk/paper/htm

Printed and bound in China by C&C Offset Printing Ltd

To our parents.
And Sharks.

Shark Party

Reef sharks are the only animals other than humans that celebrate birthdays.

A party of reef sharks wait to surprise their friend. Note jellyfish 'birthday cake'

Danger Money

Within the highly paid ranks of shark veterinarians, the best remunerated positions are shark masseuse, shark anger management therapist and shark dentist/orthodontist.

A shark dentist fits dentures
to an elderly nurse shark

A woman and a shark,
not a mermaid

Basking For Trouble

The basking shark swims close to the surface with its mouth open, filtering plankton from some 6000 litres of water per hour. Inattentive swimmers occasionally veer into the path of this gentle giant, and for a moment may find themselves lodged between its jaws, before being sneezed out again. These rare occurrences are reckoned to be the basis of most of the 35 mermaid sightings reported globally each year.

Wild At Heart

Actor Nicolas Cage's middle name is Shark.

Cage: Shark by name

An artist applies a safety kitten to a new board

Catpower

One of the greatest mysteries of the shark is its pathological fear of the kitten. A kitten's scent, its plaintive meow or even the briefest glimpse of one is enough to get most sharks hurrying in the opposite direction.

A pilot scheme in Australia to prevent shark attacks on surfers by having photographs of kittens printed on the underside of all new surfboards has met with large-scale opposition from surfers, who believe it makes them look like 'megadorks'.

Ancient Greek Sharkcher
(shark-archer)

In The Feline Of Fire

The arrow shark is the only flammable shark. Its skin is covered in an oily resin that may be set on fire. The ancient Greeks knew of this property and would shoot flaming arrow sharks on to enemy decks during battles at sea. As a defence against such attacks most ships carried kittens onboard, and would fire baskets of them back at the Greeks. This is believed to be the derivation of the word *catapult*.

Nice Day For A Great White Wedding

Australian Mercedes Gage claims to have fallen in love with a great white shark while taking photographs for a science journal off the Gold Coast in 1996. 'Our eyes met through the bars of the protective cage and I felt something very real and primal take place inside my body,' said Mercedes. She returns to visit Dylan weekly, luring him to her boat with home-made chum. Gage spends the time between visits planning their wedding, and says she is '99.999% sure' it is the same shark returning to the boat each week.

She has been in love twice before, once with River Phoenix and once with a very serious horse.

Mercedes Gage displays her scuba veil in front of a shrine to Dylan

Uruguayan coastguards sift through debris of the Sharks/Jets/sharks/jet tragedy

I Feel Pretty Hungry

The musical *West Side Story* concerns the rivalry of two gangs on the streets of New York: the Sharks and the Jets. Unfortunately neither group were helped by their namesakes when, on the 1969 tour of South America, the jet engines failed on the cast and crew's aeroplane off the coast of Uruguay, and they were all devoured by whitetip sharks.

Frankie Says Refax

The oceans' rarest shark is the fax machine shark, so called because of its distinctive nose and the beeping noise it makes as it swims. The animals were more common during the 1990s, but stocks have declined sharply in the new millennium.

The fax machine shark

Clean As A Whistle

The inside of a shark's anus has fewer germs than the human mouth.

Han-Gan Chong, 92, lost an arm, but saved his life when he thrust a can of Coke into a tiger shark's mouth in 1979. He has been the face of Coca-Cola in China since the attack

Boom, Shark Shark Shark The Room

Sharks can withstand many substances that are poisonous to humans, including arsenic and strychnine. However, if a shark is fed even the smallest amount of Coca-Cola, it will explode.

One Man And His Dogfish

The original shark cages were intended to hold sharks captive while humans swam safely around them. These devices required the employment of a *shark corraller*. Using a trained dogfish and a combination of whistling and arm movements, a skilled corraller could round up all sharks in the vicinity and have the dogfish 'drive' them into a single shark cage, which would be kept closed until the area was clear of humans.

Shark corralling is one of the three professions considered to be a 'true calling'. The others are the priesthood and puppeteering.

Legendary shark corraller Len Fricker signals to his dogfish Martina

Am I Hot Or Not?

The goblin shark has been scientifically proven to be the ugliest living creature. Therapists often use pictures of the goblin shark to give prospective cosmetic surgery patients a sense of perspective.

You're never as ugly
as a goblin shark

I'm Dreaming Of A Great White Christmas

Steven Spielberg's feature film *Jaws* was never released in Greece. As a result, sharks are not feared in this country, but are an integral part of the Greek tourism industry. It is estimated that 25% of Greek tourism revenue comes from sharks, including shark rides, shark petting and shark taxis.

On the island of Corfu, Christmas presents are delivered not by Santa Claus, but by Ozzie, the Great White Shark of Generosity.

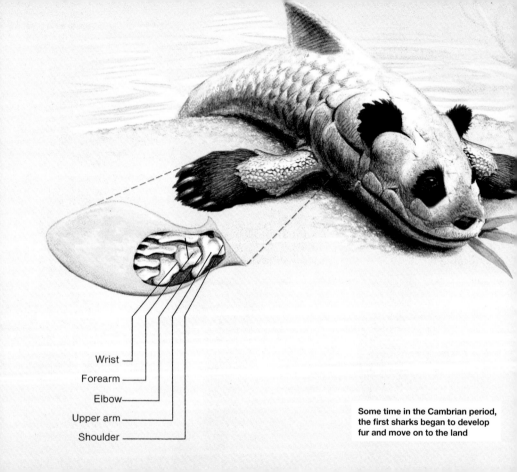

Wrist
Forearm
Elbow
Upper arm
Shoulder

Some time in the Cambrian period,
the first sharks began to develop
fur and move on to the land

DNAww/Aaargh!

Genetically, the land animal that the great white shark most closely resembles is the giant panda. Their digestive tract and cerebral cortex are almost identical, and the two share a common ancestor in the zebra trilobite. Around 300 million years ago, a single gene mutated into an *adorable* and a *ferocious* form, and the two separate species began to evolve.

Live Long And Prosper

Such was the public terror and hysteria created in Victorian London by Mary Shelley's follow-up horror novel to *Frankenstein*, the authorities took the decision to buy up all of the remaining copies of *Prosper, the Invisible Flying Vampire Shark* and dump them into the Thames.

PROSPER
The Invisible Flying Vampyre Shark

By the glymmer of the half-extinguished light, I saw the dull, yellow eye of the creature open; it breathed hard; and a convulsive motion agitated its limbs. ... I rushed out of the room.

Page 43.

F. Brler, del.   W. Chevalier, sculp.

The only existing page of the book

The giraffe shark is born with a 2-metre-long neck

Packed To The Giraffters

At over 6 metres, the giraffe shark is the longest shark on earth. It is also the only shark with eyelashes.

Dangerous Games

Prior to advances in chemical engineering during the 1950s, children's modelling clay Play-Doh was made from processed tiger shark brain. This explains the high price of the product – at certain times it was more expensive per ounce than gold – and the tiny quantities children got to play with. Thirty-eight Play-Doh hunters died harvesting their bounty between 1920 and 1949.

**Children playing with the
three original Play-Doh
colours: medulla, cortex
and pituitary**

Spurtains For You

At birth, the oceanic whitetip shark is perfectly proportioned, but less than 5 centimetres in length. It remains this size for one week before growing a staggering 2–3 metres in a single day. Many home aquarium owners have mistaken the baby oceanic whitetip for the miniature teabag shark, and have woken up to find a fully grown man-eating shark thrashing around their lounge.

Most home insurance plans do not include cover for unexpected shark growth

Smirky Water

Sharks are the only animals with no sense of humour whatsoever. Although they are occasionally glimpsed smiling, this is reckoned to coincide with nostalgic reminiscences about gruesome murders they have committed in the past.

A great white remembers an atrocity

The texting sharks of Lisbon

OMG

The electromagnetic brainwaves of the reef shark make it the only animal that can send telephone text messages with its mind. Random messages received by visitors to the Lisbon aquarium have included: 'ROFLOL', 'xoxxo' and the ominous : (

shark

Shark My Words

The etymology of the word shark is the subject of much debate among sharkeologists. Some believe it is derived from the Arabic *sh'aak* meaning 'nightmare death submarine'. Others believe it comes from the Aboriginal word *sharriji* meaning 'ungrateful friend'. Some scholars believe it may derive its name from the fact that these specific letters, when put in that order, look quite like a shark.

Sharks: Not As Bad As Nazis

Hitler saw sharks as nature's embodiment of his Nazi ideal: a ruthlessly efficient master race that ruled the blue planet. However, sharks proved reluctant to participate in his propaganda. In a demonstration at the Munich Rally of 1937 of how stronger races are supposed to overwhelm weaker ones, a shoal of tuna were dropped into a huge glass tank containing Patrick and Natasha, a pair of 3-metre blue sharks branded with the swastika. Perhaps due to the ill-treatment they had already received or maybe sensing pity for the tuna fish, the sharks refused to cooperate and instead befriended their tank-mates, sharing food and allowing them to ride around on their backs.

A furious Hitler later had them taken out and shot.

24

Multi-Storey Car Shark

Statistically, you are 50 times more likely to be in a car accident on the way to the beach than attacked by a shark while swimming there. Spare a thought then for Lars Muller of Munich who, while driving to East Pomerania Beach in Germany in 1993, was hit by a truck carrying Gertie, a 300-kilo nurse shark bound for the Cologne aquarium. The truck's brakes failed at an intersection and struck Muller's vehicle from the side, cracking the animal's transportation tank and ejecting Gertie, along with 500 litres of her tank's seawater, and depositing them through his sunroof.

Although he managed to escape unharmed, the same cannot be said of the aquarium, which received a bill of 3000 Deutschmarks for shark removal and car valeting.

HÄLT

Emergency services are reluctant to assist this accident victim

Many Eastern European
nativity scenes still feature
the Shark of Nazareth

Shark The Herald Angels Sing

For many centuries it was Christian doctrine that a shark was present at the birth of Jesus Christ. Indeed, the image of the Shark of Nazareth appears in many medieval illuminated manuscripts, and, in the Dark Ages, the existence of an air-breathing land shark was seen by Christians as further proof of the miraculous power of God. Recent studies show that the source of the belief may have been the similarity of the ancient Aramaic words for *shark* and *bucket*.

The Shark Whisperer

Like most overly aggressive creatures, the shark suffers from very low self-esteem. However, with self-confidence therapy this problem can be treated, and *bad* sharks may be turned *good*. Marine psychologist Dr Ravi Darcy is the world leader in this field and has recently opened Dr Ravi's Happy Shark Village in Sri Lanka. Here, former man-eaters put on shows for the public, bouncing balls on their noses, jumping through hoops and allowing children to put their heads into their mouths.

Dr Ravi's Happy Shark Village

Pro-shark-hunting image that has been doctored by the Japanese government

KONICHIWHAAAT???

Even though one-third of all shark species face extinction, spurious reasons are often given by governments to justify their continued commercial fishing. Recently Japan has tried to maintain that if shark catches were reduced by even 10%, the Indian Ocean would become so thick with fish it would be impossible to go swimming.

A Shark To Remember

Following the sinking of the *Titanic* in April 1914, her owners, the White Star Line, circulated a report that sharks had bitten the holes that sank the doomed ship. Had this bizarre suggestion gained support, it would have absolved the owners of any legal responsibility for the ship's demise and the subsequent loss of life, as the fine print in the construction contract had stated, 'We will build an unsinkable ship.'*

* 'But under no circumstances will it be shark proof.'

PEL REGNO ESTERO
Anno . . . . . L. 5 — L. 10 —
Semestre . . . » 2,50 » 5 —

Si pubblica a Milano ogni Domenica
Supplemento illustrato del " Corriere della Sera „

Uffici del giornale:
Via Solferino, N. 28
MILANO

Per tutti gli articoli e illustrazioni è riservata la proprietà artistica e letteraria, secondo le leggi e i trattati internazionali.

Anno XIV — Num. 17.   28 Aprile - 5 Maggio 1912.   Centesimi 10 il numero.

Terribile disastro marittimo : il più grande transatlantico " Titanic „ affonda con 1600 persone nell'Oceano spezzato da un iceberg.

The story gained great traction
with the Italian media

The Great White Escape

The best-known method of repelling an attack by a great white shark is to try and poke the animal directly in the eyes. If you are lucky, this will cause it to recoil and it could lose interest in finishing you off. However, the species has several other weaknesses that may also be exploited.

1) The great white is notoriously ticklish around the pelvic fin. Find the correct spot and it will roll on to its back with a look of benign ecstasy on its face.

2) Try to embrace the animal around the gills – great whites hate inter-species intimacy.

3) If possible, place headphones over the shark's head and select a Charlie Parker or Louis Armstrong track. Great whites hate jazz.

A diver enrages a great white with the harmonic experimentation of the Brad Mehldau Trio

Dwayne Tandy celebrates his first birthday back on land

Dwayne's World, Sharky Time, Excellent

In November 1970, an 18-month-old boy was swept overboard by a freak wave while on a shark-spotting cruise with his mother off Adelaide, South Australia.

Eight years later the now nine-year-old was caught in a fisherman's net at Port Lincoln, several hundred kilometres up the coast. He was alive, but deeply unhappy to be leaving the water. Dwayne Tandy is reckoned to be the only person ever raised by sharks.

He is now head of Adelaide City Council's parking fines and car clamping department.

Fin Here To Eternity

Despite its fearsome reputation, the great white shark is one of the most romantic animals of the sea. As part of his courtship ritual, the male is known to take the female on a series of dates to hear whale song and shower her with gifts of dead seals and surfers' legs.

Since the 1960s, marine biologists have observed pairs of great whites lying closely together on the ocean floor. Initially they assumed the sharks were ill or sleeping, but once it was discovered that the sharks were on their side with overlapping pectoral fins, it was determined that they were spooning. Great whites sometimes spoon for weeks at a time.

A great white couple enjoy a barbershop of beluga whales

Lucky Ducker

Landlocked Luxembourg's only ever shark attack took place in July 1978 when a 2-foot bull shark, which had escaped from Wasserbillig Aquarium into the national sewerage system, made its way up a series of pipes into the 5th floor apartment of landscape gardener Anton Fignon. He was on his toilet at the time, contemplating a cryptic crossword. Despite suffering deep lacerations to the exposed area, he managed to subdue the fugitive animal using an electric toothbrush and a bottle of bleach. He would later adopt him, keeping Lucas in a large tank in his sitting room.

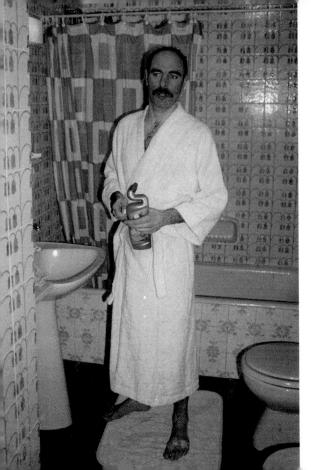

Anton Fignon with the bleach that saved his life

The red and white of the
South African lifeguards

Red, White And Chew

A swimmer in gingham swimwear has never been attacked by a shark. It is for this reason that South African beach lifeguards all wear gingham.

Charlie Garber is saved by a whale shark on a beach in Western Australia

Good For What Whales You

Statistically the least dangerous shark is the enormous whale shark, which has a global all-time fatalities total of minus four. That is, four times, drowning swimmers have been inadvertently saved by one of these inattentive giants accidentally poking them back inshore.

The Sweetest Revenge

The world's smallest shark is the sugar-cube shark, which is just 3 centimetres in length. Although diminutive in size, the animals are just as ferocious as their larger cousins.

Recently deciphered hieroglyphics reveal that a favourite trick of Aztec assassins was to slip a sugar-cube shark into the victims' hot chocolate and dance around as they were devoured from within.

A diver gets dangerously
close to a sugar-cube shark

Hopeful students line up to see if they have been accepted on a Floridian Sharkeology course

ALL OTHER NOTICES

SHARKEOLOGY FACULTY NOTICES

Miami Advice

The explosion in the number of shark documentaries being produced in the last ten years has hugely increased worldwide demand for sharksperts (shark experts). In response, the University of Florida has introduced the first full-time sharkeology degree. The course has been so popular, it has resulted in a significant drain on other more traditional vocational studies. Florida currently has the developed world's lowest proportion of qualified doctors per 1000 people (0.3) and highest proportion of sharksperts (28), meaning that if a Floridian is attacked by a shark, his or her family is likely to be very well informed about the incident, but the person attacked will most likely die from their injuries.

Mistaken Dentity

Estimating its size from tooth fossils discovered in the 1970s, sharkeologists of the time concluded that Megalodon, the prehistoric dinosaur shark, would have been over 30 metres long. However, today some experts believe that Megalodon may have been the same size as one of today's great white sharks, just with enormous teeth.

Artists' impressions of
Megalodon from 1976 (left)
and today (right)

Illustration from Dutch government information leaflet *Stay Safe around Sharks*

Stat Attack

Nine out of ten shark attacks take place in water. Of the other 10%, the most common scenarios are on the decks of fishing boats, stuffed sharks falling from their mountings and crushing people in museums, and people falling out of bed during shark-based nightmares.

Mocking The Week

In Ivory Coast, Shark Week refers to the sombre annual seven-day memorial that commemorates the death in 1978 of 11 schoolchildren and their bus driver when they veered off a cliff and were devoured by bull sharks. When the Discovery Channel started publicising its own Shark Week in late 2003, the Ivorian government fined the station $US12 million for insensitivity, and banned it from ever broadcasting in Ivory Coast again.

Pope John Paul II attends a Mass during Ivory Coast Shark Week in full ceremonial robes

Mayor Pelmet poses in his mayoral chain of office

Shark Night-Mayor

In an attempt to attract tourists to the town of Mulraney, Rhode Island, in the mid-1980s, Mayor Grover Pelmet renamed it Mulraney: Shark Capital of the World. The problem with this claim was that not a single shark had been spotted in the waters off the town in the previous hundred years, so single-handedly Pelmet began a campaign to attract sharks to the area. He secured bags of rancid sausages to the underside of boats in the harbour and even attempted to fit rubber shark-fin prosthetics to the family of dolphins who lived in the bay in the hope that it would attract other 'sharks'.

His exertions began to take a toll on his mental health, and the last straw came when his wife found him 10 metres off Mulraney Strand late one night covered in gravy shouting, 'Hello, boys, I'm a lady shark.' He retired from the mayorship soon after.

The turnip field where Roland Silverstein's 'shark' was 'caught'

Turnip And Tucker

Notorious celebrity chef Roland Silverstein attracted the ire of conservationists when he put great white shark ravioli on the menu of Famine, his exclusive London eatery, in 1997. After a storm of bad publicity, most of it centring on Silverstein's claim to have caught the endangered animal himself, he was forced to admit that the pasta didn't really contain shark, but processed turnip.

His barbecued cheetah was subsequently found to be chicken and his fried panda was in fact tofu cooked in KitKats.

Bats And Balls

Across time, different parts of the shark have been put to a variety of uses. Shark teeth have been used in jewellery, as arrowheads and as the taps on the soles of tap-dancing shoes. Aside from being used in soup, shark fins have been painted yellow and used as road signs, hung in wardrobes as coat hangers and were the orginal table tennis bats. Due to their durability and bounce, shark eyes were often used as table tennis balls and today are still a common replacement prosthetic gonad in men who have suffered testicular cancer.

Sudanese women play the original ping-pong, known as 'pata pata'

Kiss Of Death

The make-out shark dwells in the tropical waters of the Pacific Ocean. It is similar in appearance to the great white shark, but has no teeth and feeds only on krill. The make-out shark is a curious and friendly animal that investigates other creatures by rubbing its mouth up against them, hence its name.

Despite having no desire or ability to eat humans, the make-out shark has been responsible for more deaths than its carnivorous cousin, as encounters with them usually result in heart attacks.

The make-out shark
scores another victim

Greg Norman: not an actual shark

Fore!

Australian golfer Greg Norman is nicknamed the Great White Shark. Most people assume this is due to his Australian nationality and blond hair, but the name dates to a dark period in his early twenties when Norman, having been struck on the head by a ball at the 1972 New South Wales Open, believed he was a shark and terrorised swimmers off the beaches of far North Queensland for a summer.

Sharktistical Analysis

New research from the University of Cape Town indicates that the average ocean swimmer devotes 12% of their thoughts to their swimming stroke, 4% to whether their swimming attire is still in position, and 84% to whether they are about to be attacked by a shark.

The average pool swimmer has the same three preoccupations, although the average concern about a shark attack is slightly lower.

Thoughts of Ocean Swimmer

%

100

80 — 84%

60

40

20 — 12%

4%

0

Swimming Stroke · Swimming Attire · Shark Attack

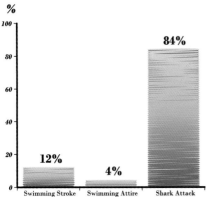

Thoughts of Pool Swimmer

%

100

80

60

40 — 45%

27% · 28%

20

0

Swimming Stroke · Swimming Attire · Shark Attack

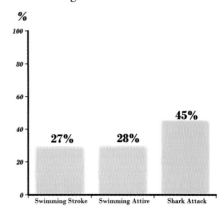

A traditional Jewish wedding in Greenland

Sharkspah!

Sharks freeze solid at minus 29 degrees Celsius. Once frozen, a shark is very brittle and will shatter easily. This is reckoned to be the most humane way to destroy a shark.

The ceremonial smashing of the shark is a tradition at Jewish weddings in polar regions. The bride and groom throw the frozen shark off the roof of the synagogue, symbolising that, together, their love can smash a shark.

Not Great Expectations

Until 1947, the name of every species of shark was prefixed with the adjective *great*. That was until the public relations firms representing the Great Wall of China, the Great Barrier Reef and Great Britain mounted a legal challenge, claiming that this made people unfairly associate them with sharks. The International High Court ruled in favour of the plaintiffs, although, fearing repercussions perhaps, they deemed that the great white shark could retain its prefix – a remarkable legal precedent given that sharks had no representation in the case.

Court illustration from *The People* v. *Sharks*

'GREAT'

Hot dog vendors,
Yankee Stadium 1965

Bread And Butts

Between 1962 and 1968, all hot dogs sold at Yankee Stadium were made from shark meat. Pig numbers had rapidly decreased along the east coast of the United States as a result of an outbreak of Blue Eye disease. Once the pig population's numbers were restored, hot dog manufacturers returned to the original recipe of pig lips, eyelids and ani.

Sharkira

In the 1930s, low literacy levels in Colombia led the government to introduce one shark per school to be used as a tool to encourage children to learn to read. The threat of being fed to or even just made to stand beside the school shark resulted in a generation of diligent students, including 1982 Nobel Prize Winner Gabriel Garcia Marquez. Unfortunately, this generation also suffered from abnormally high anxiety-related conditions. Garcia Marquez is rumoured to have written his epic novel *100 Years of Solitude* in a sleepless two-week frenzy of writing in 1966.

When Colombian singer Shakira is struggling to finish a song, she purportedly uses a technique taught to her by her father of imagining there is a shark in the corner. This is believed to account for the numerous distressed yelps she includes in her songs.

Colombian schoolroom, 1936

Fisherman Raul Delgado displays his non-vintage headwear

Berserk Warriors

There is much debate as to the lifespan of the shark with some experts estimating 60 to 80 years, while others put the figure much higher than this. The argument was temporarily blown apart by the discovery of a Viking helmet in the stomach of a mature hammerhead shark caught in the Gulf of Mexico in 1986. Could a shark really have lived for a thousand years? The mystery was solved some months later when a telephone number was found written on the inside of the helmet and it was traced to Patrick Bamford, a fan of the Minnesota Vikings American football team, who had thrown it into the sea after his team lost to the New Orleans Saints in a play-off.

Sharkbreak Hotel

The great white that was seen in the real shark footage in *Jaws* was the first shark ever to get a Hollywood acting agent. After the film's international success, Mitzi, the South Australian shark, was signed to Michael Curran Management. Despite auditioning for many films, including *Free Willy* and the 1998 telemovie adaptation of *Moby Dick*, Mitzi has never secured another leading role. He can briefly be seen in the background of an episode of *Seaquest DSV*, in which he played Large Fish #2.

MITZI

M. Curran Management
0052 558901

Eye Colour:Black   Weight:480lbs
Hair Colour:N/A   Shoulder Width:N/A
Height: N/A   Waist:157"

The real Jaws

Ocular repulsion and attraction
in two bourbon sharks

Eye-nimal Magnetism

The hammerhead shark is not a species of shark, but rather any species of shark suffering from a condition known as *ocular repulsion*. Any severe trauma to the head of the shark can cause the realignment of the electrons in the shark's eyeballs. This results in the eyeballs becoming magnetised. Because both eye-balls possess the same polarity, they repel, resulting in a hammerhead shark. Much more rare are sharks whose eyes have positive attraction. Such cases result in the pinhead shark.

Complete Bull

Celebrities frequently claim to have been involved in shark attacks in order to toughen up their public image. In 1995, vocal group Color Me Badd claimed to have been set upon by bull sharks as they swam at Glenelg beach, South Australia. According to group member Donnie Wetherspoon, 'We formed a human diamond and sang till we had calmed them down.' The incident gained the group much publicity, especially as it coincided with the release of their *No Bull* remix album. However, drama turned to scandal when marine biologists pointed out that bull sharks are not found in this region, and the group was forced to admit to fans that they can't even swim.

Color Me Badd appear outside the hospital following their 'ordeal'. Note member Kevin Thornton (second from right) pretending he has lost two fingers

A blue shark enjoying
the respite of some air

H2ow

The reason sharks often swim with their dorsal fin out of the water is because this fin is allergic to salt. When submerged, the fin is very itchy but air has a soothing effect on the irritation. This constant state of discomfort is one of the reasons why sharks are always so angry.

Sharke Diem

When different shark species arrive at the same feeding ground, they line up in alphabetical order of Latin name to take turns eating. Scientists have no adequate explanation for this behaviour.

The alphabetical intra-species organisation of sharks

1. **Wobbegong**
(*Apristurus spongiceps*)
2. **Lurker shark**
(*Brachaelurus lurki*)
3. **Cashew shark**
(*Cephaloscyllium stephenrocheus*)
4. **Black-tipped reef shark**
(*Dalatias doomsnackerus*)
5. **Whale shark**
(*Etmopterus enormi*)
6. **Leopard shark**
(*Googolia filesharaari*)
7. **Thresher shark**
(*Heterodontus swishaswisha*)
8. **Carrot shark**
(*Pseudoginglymostoma pointiorangeum*)
9. **Basking shark**
(*Triakis megapplianceus*)

Das Booted To Bits

Robert Fulton's first design for his submarine in 1800 had the crew of two lying inside a hollowed-out shark, fitted with a front window with curtains. At the only test of *Carcharhinus*, as he named the craft, it was kicked to pieces by anxious bathers as it attempted to land at a beach near Bordeaux, France.

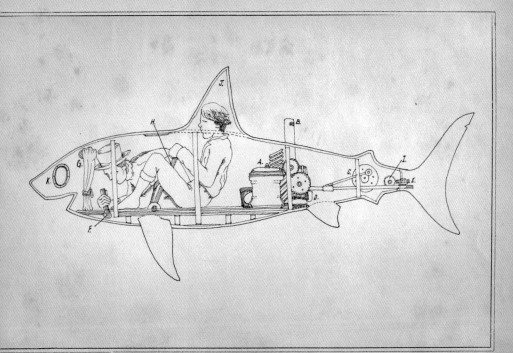

by H.B.Barlow.   Published 1st July, 1800.   C.F.Cheffins Lithog.

PERSPECTIVE VIEW OF FULTON'S MACHINE

The original submarine

Gerry Rafferty's saxophonist
Raphael Ravenscroft solos on
his favourite shark, Rosemary

Smooth Chomperator

Blowing into the mouth of a recently deceased mako shark produces a sound remarkably similar to that of the alto saxophone. By controlling the air pressure through the gills, the pitch can be altered. The refrain from Gerry Rafferty's 1978 hit 'Baker Street' is played on a mako, as is the theme to 1980s police drama *Cagney and Lacey* and all of Sade's hits.

Monster Of The Sleep

Sharks continue to move during sleep, except during lunar eclipses. On these rare occasions, they cluster together on the sea floor and sleep in 'shark piles'. Shark piles can consist of between 12 and 400 animals.

The safety afforded by having so many of the ocean's apex predators asleep at once allows more vulnerable sea creatures to behave with uncharacteristic abandon. During lunar eclipses crustaceans are known to remove their shells and perform elaborate dances with sea horses and turtles.

A shark pile

Professional shark hunter Greg Woodburne proudly displays his reunion name tag

20ᵀᴴ REUNION
88
Greg Woodburne
Profession: Shark Hunter

The Secret Of My Sharkcess

Studies show that at school reunions, shark hunter is the second most impressive profession to have. The most impressive profession is freelance shark hunter.

Adult Entertainment

The first public television broadcasts were aired in Schenectady, New York, in 1927. There were three programmes in the inaugural schedule. From 6am to 12pm, an image of a balloon constituted children's programming, from 12pm to 6pm, a film of a rose in a field was directed at female viewers, and from 6 to 6.15pm footage of a shark swimming in circles in a tank was broadcast strictly for adults only. In 1928, a programme specifically for men was introduced. It consisted of a close-up of a firing rifle.

Adult television *circa* 1929

Plant And Animals

Led Zeppelin guitarist Jimmy Page used shark teeth as his guitar plec-trums throughout the 1970s. For this purpose he had a full-grown bull shark named Mr Chompy transported around the world with the band. As tensions between Page and lead singer Robert Plant grew throughout the decade, Plant insisted on having his own, slightly larger Greenland shark that he called The May Queen in a tank backstage.

Upon hearing of Led Zeppelin's sharks, Queen lead singer Freddie Mercury had a killer whale named Beelzebub added to his group's touring rider.

Plant relaxes with The May Queen. He would take her out of her tank for 15 minutes each day

The *Gentle Waft* hummus spill, 1978
Inset: Sharks still visit the wreck to gorge

62

Things That Make You Go Hummus

Given the choice, most man-eating sharks would actually prefer a veg-etarian option. In 1978 when the hummus-transporting tanker the *Gentle Waft* broke up on rocks off Gary Point, South Africa, the five-man crew was soon surrounded by whitetip and great white sharks. As the three women and two men waited to be devoured, they noticed the animals heading instead in the direction of the ship's leaking hummus tank. Al-most immediately the sharks' demeanour changed from aggression to concern for the welfare of the struggling sailors. After six hours feasting on the hummus, the sharks delivered the crew inshore to safety, giving them a ride on their dorsal fins.

Jaws Of Death

The record number of separate shark attacks on a single person is 12, on Pete Benchley, a taxi driver from Cape Cod, Massachusetts, who happens to share his name with the author of the bestselling novel and later film, *Jaws*.

Following an attack in the early 1970s the author does not swim in the sea any more; however, he was involved in an incident at the Melbourne Aquarium in 1990 when the facility's 14 sharks simultaneously rammed the viewing tube as he walked through it. Nobody was injured in the incident, but the thought-to-be unbreakable glass was cracked.

Not the author of *Jaws*

PETE
THE SURVIVOR
BENCHLEY
8002222

Sammy, 1971, the nightmare begins

My Shark Will Go On

The least successful government information slogan of all time is the Canadian government's 1971 'Sammy the shark will help you cross the road' campaign. Unfortunately its launch coincided with several high-profile shark attacks on the nation's beaches and Canadian children simply refused to cross the road. School attendance plummeted and the government was forced to launch a new campaign with the slogan, 'Sammy is dead, children, everything is OK now.' To this day Montrealer Celine Dion will only cross roads at great speed.

Crazy, Sexy, Tool

A group of hammerhead sharks with over 12 members is called a toolbox. Under 12 is called a toolbelt.

A group of great white sharks is called a catastrophe.

A toolbox, a toolbelt and a catastrophe

Pacific Lotion

The chances of being attacked by a shark at the beach are around 268 million to one. These odds drop to about 100 million to one at certain beaches where shark attacks have taken place in the past, and to 20 million to one if you add in certain other factors such as time of day, time of year and whether you are swimming alone. In the 1970s the odds of an attack dropped to around 1000 to one for swimmers wearing Ambre Solaire's short-lived lasagne-flavoured suncream.

French magazine ad for the potentially lethal sunblock

Fishermen would often dress as women in an attempt to outwit the Galapagos shark

Ow De Toilette

The Galapagos shark can be described as the only truly man-eating shark, as all 46 attacks on humans recorded in the last 50 years have been on men. It is believed to be attracted to the scent of certain aftershaves.

The bikini shark, on the other hand, targets only female bathers, snapping off their swimwear, which it later uses as dental floss.

Air-Whale Special

Whale sharks have an airtight stomach, meaning that, when out of water, the animals may be inflated to 10 times their already enormous size. They were commonly used in airship construction in the early part of the last century.

Bavarian aristocrat Baron von Daimler travelled the world in his shark airship known as the *Findenburgh*

**Lucky one-armed canoeist
Peter Logan**

Manatee Performance

There is evidence that sharks feel pangs of remorse following attacks on humans. When a tiger shark removed the left arm of canoeist Peter Logan off Florida in 1986, it soon discovered that the arm was prosthetic, Logan having suffered the injury in a car accident the previous year. An hour later, the shark reappeared at the beach to deposit the arm on the shore along with a peace offering of a dead manatee.

Donnie Sharko

Globally more people are killed annually by kittens, chandeliers and cotton buds than by sharks.

Kitten suffocation victim Britt McCamey with her assailant Cuddle Pumpkin

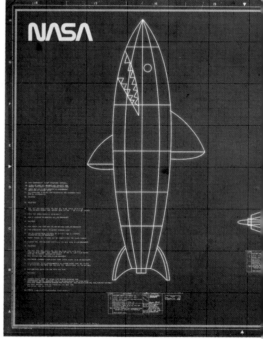

Dr Shark found NASA's designs
'Unnnacceptabubble!'

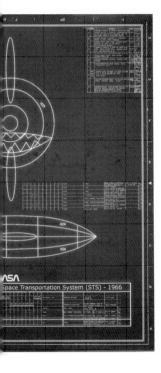

Shark Side Of The Moon

Owing to its dynamic shape, if dropped from an aeroplane, a shark will glide to earth, landing gently on its belly.

NASA's earliest designs for its space shuttle copied the shape of the shark, but the design had to be dropped when a legal challenge was mounted from Marvel Comics over its resemblance to the design of Evil Dr Shark's Sharksporter from its SharkWorld series.

Grandfather Thorpe with Ian and Sister Wendy

Pool Shark

Australian swimming legend Ian Thorpe's grandfather had a novel way of training his grandson. He would hide a piece of raw steak in the pocket of Ian's swimming shorts, and release the family's small grey nurse shark Sister Wendy into the family pool as Ian completed his lengths. It was only years later that Thorpe learned that Sister Wendy had been de-toothed and was just being friendly. This explains Thorpe's career-long habit of jumping straight out of the pool and sprinting to the car park in tears at the end of every race.

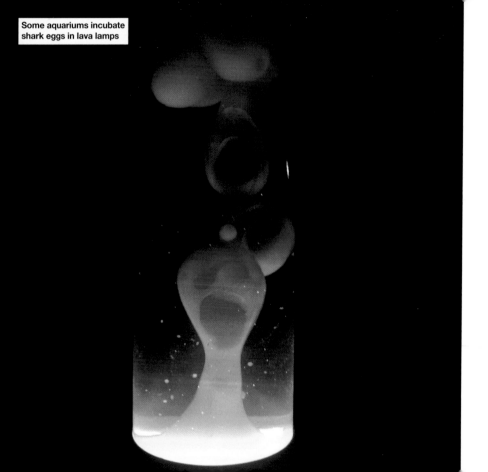

Some aquariums incubate
shark eggs in lava lamps

Waters Of Life

In addition to seawater, sharks can live and breathe happily in all of the following liquids – diesel, flat lemonade, lava lamp lava, flubber and stock.

Sharktography

In the Second World War, British intelligence operatives tried sending covert messages to America written in paint on the sides of migratory sharks. Unfortunately German spies learned of the plan and intercepted the sharks, changing the messages slightly. Thus 'Japanese planning to attack' arrived as 'Japanese planning to convert their attics' and instead of warning Pearl Harbor, the military placed an embargo on roof insulation materials into Japan.

US Marines deciphering
sharks off Nantucket, 1943

I'm With Stupid

Although a vital source of vitamin C when cooked and eaten, the dunce shark was regarded by eighteenth-century mariners as the stupidest and most pointless of all sea creatures. The animals were forever leaping out of the sea on to the decks of ships, or getting stuck in anchor chains. The tradition arose of removing the shark's long dorsal fin and the dimmest crew member being made to wear it as a hat. Ironically this led to the demise of dunce shark stocks and a spike in scurvy among sailors.

An illustration from the original account of the mutiny on the *Bounty*, showing a dunce hat

BOUNTY

Scientists bring a whale shark back to its pristine state

Fade To Grey

Most sharks are born white, but gradually turn grey as sediment from the ocean builds up on their skin. They can be returned to their natural white colour if they are cleaned correctly, but cleaning a shark is laborious. It requires:

1) tranquilliser gun

2) shark muzzle (or a very large steel bin if a shark muzzle is unavailable)

3) 200 litres bleach/soda water/lemon juice

4) 2000 litres warm soapy water

5) 500 loofahs

The Man With The Golden Shark

Recording artist R. Kelly was fined $3 million by the American Society for the Prevention of Cruelty to Animals when it emerged that Tooth, the small, gold reef shark he'd been carrying with him in a glass briefcase full of water to after-parties, fragrance launches and premieres for two years, was actually a series of different sharks. Each one had perished after a single outing, poisoned by the gold paint Kelly's personal assistant had applied to it.

R. Kelly with one of his Tooths

Braiders Of The Lost Shark

Sharks in aquariums often grow hair on top of their head. It is actually a form of algae that appears due to the lack of natural currents in tanks. The material can be removed, but if a specialist shark barber isn't available, aquarium staff may choose to braid it into an unobtrusive style.

A captive shark with cornrows

George Lazenby recuperates on-set with co-star Diana Rigg

Dr Toe

In a scene in the James Bond film *On Her Majesty's Secret Service*, actor George Lazenby was supposed to water-ski from the back of a nuclear submarine while standing on two live sharks and holding co-star Diana Rigg. Two lemon sharks were selected for the stunt – a normally placid species with no recorded history of violence towards humans. However, as the day of filming progressed and the scene was captured from various angles, Bond's left ski grew hungry and took an opportunistic chomp at 007's loafer, removing the tip of it and the top joints of his two smallest toes. The injury halted filming for two weeks and ensured that although Lazenby may not go down in history as the best Bond he is certainly the one that leaned to the side the most.

Shark Off

In Tok Pisin, the most widely spoken language in Papua New Guinea, *shark* is the most offensive possible curse word.

Papua New Guinean children enjoy some satirical graffiti

Shell-Sharked

The least dangerous animal in all of mythology is the Tortark – a beast with the head of a shark and the body of a tortoise. Although the animal could potentially remove your arm in a single bite, it would take up to an hour to cross the room to get to you.

Mythical beast the Tortark

Making The Earth Move

The painting of shark heads on the front of missiles and torpedoes has been banned by the US military since the 1970s, following several incidents where sharks attempted to mate with unexploded devices that had come to rest on the seabed.

US airmen inadvertently endangering
the lives of their Navy comrades

**Daniel Day Lewis
recovers from his
shark incarceration**

There Will Be Sharks

Brazilian fishermen were astonished to find the actor Daniel Day Lewis alive inside a great white shark caught off Rio in 1998. The star of *My Left Foot* was in a suit of armour, using scuba apparatus to breathe. He had allowed himself to be swallowed by the shark five days before in order to prepare for his vocal role as Mr Sharky T. Shark in the upcoming animated children's film *Mr Sharky's Awfully Big Ad-FIN-ture*.

Pythagoras never forgave
himself for the shark attack
that killed his brothers

Don't Believe The Hypotenuse

Mathematician Pythagoras came up with his most famous theorem when he observed the triangular dorsal fin of a tiger shark break the surface of the water at Crotone, southern Italy. As he feverishly scribbled the details of his proof in the sand, he failed to observe the shark devouring his two brothers.

Sniff'rent Strokes

Such is the phenomenal sense of smell of sharks that they are increasingly trained by border patrol authorities to sniff out drugs in airports. These sniffer sharks are wheeled around airports in tanks by handlers known as sharkotics officers.

Daphne, Vancouver airport's border protection shark, monitors the main baggage carousel from her wall-tank

George Brennan, his son Luke and the late Betty (portrait)

Chomp And Ceremony

Until the 1950s, shark jaws were often used as dentures. Florida's George Brennan had the unique claim of using the same set of teeth to chew his food that had eaten his wife, Betty.

Everyfin In Its Right Place

In the first three years of their career, influential rock band Radiohead were called Shark Pit. They wore shark costumes onstage and only sang songs about life as undersea predators. For two years, between being called Shark Pit and Radiohead, they were called Hell Toupee.

Immaculate Sharkception

The female hammerhead shark can become pregnant without any input from a male if she feels that the time is right to have a baby.

The 'hammerhead defence', as it became known, was used by numerous English women as an explanation to their returning husbands after the Second World War.

Private Timothy Key returns home to meet 'miracle' baby Brooklyn

The unique anatomy of the
female portbeagle shark

They Never Had A Chance

The female portbeagle shark has its birthing canal at the top of its dorsal fin, so that at birth, its offspring are shot vertically up to 10 metres into the air. An unlucky seagull flying overhead can easily become baby's first meal.

Stuck On You

The sello shark is the world's most adhesive shark. It captures its prey by activating sticky glands and simply bumping into whatever it wishes to eat. Occasionally it encounters something too large to eat, such as a submarine or a wayward swimmer.

One-time Somali Olympic hopeful Awaale Samakab Guleed's swimming career was cut short by an encounter with two sello sharks

I'm Sharking Here!

New York's subway system is one of three public transit systems in the world open 365 days of the year. However, for 14 hours on the 24th of October, the entire system is closed for 'scheduled track maintenance'. This maintenance consists of flooding the network of tunnels and releasing Caribbean pigeye sharks to eat the rats. At the end of the 14 hours, the subways are drained and the sharks are released into the Hudson River. This method reduces the pest population by a dramatic 72% every year, but conspiracy theorists worry that it is leading to the evolution of shark-resilient mega-rats.

Times Square

Scheduled track maintenance
day, 24 October 1978

The Captain And Fin-ille

The global telephone number for the International Shark Hotline is 1800-SHARK (1800-74275). The number can be called in the event of a shark sighting or attack, but most calls are made by people who simply need to discuss their fear of sharks. The hotline is manned by volunteers, a high proportion of them retired sea captains.

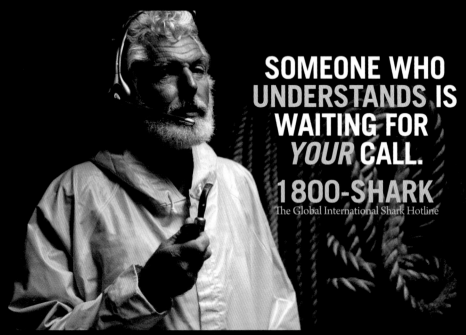

SOMEONE WHO UNDERSTANDS IS WAITING FOR *YOUR* CALL.

1800-SHARK
The Global International Shark Hotline

The Global International Shark Hotline is intended to provide general information only. Shark based sufferers should seek appropriate professional advice before taking or refraining from taking any action in reliance on any information from 1800-shark.

Shark hotline poster, featuring founder Skipper Davis Evans

La Toya Jackson relaxes in her shark tooth bathroom

Mosaicy Breaky Shark

The great white shark grows as many as 6000 teeth in its lifetime, enough to tile a 200-square-foot bathroom. Great white tooth bathrooms are a major status symbol among the ultra-rich. Lance Armstrong, Nora Ephron and Stephen Hawking all have great white bathrooms in at least one of their homes.

Jaws writer Peter Benchley had one, until the ceiling mysteriously collapsed on him as he lay in the bath in 1990 and he almost drowned.

Loud But Deadly

Scientists have finally established the reason why certain sharks leap out of the ocean, performing elaborate gymnastic twists before crashing back into the water. It had been thought to be part of a mating ritual, or perhaps a way of shaking off sea lice. In fact it is to get rid of trapped wind. Sharks are susceptible to this form of indigestion after eating pufferfish, aerosol cans and certain kelps. Great white farts are often mistaken for foghorns by boats at sea.

As it releases wind, the great white can propel itself up to 100 metres across the top of the water

A sharkstronaut fan attends a space shuttle launch

Zero Graviteeth

Of all animals that have been taken into space, sharks are the least useful. Their compact internal organs stand them in good stead when it comes to dealing with the lack of gravity, but their desire to eat through cables and kill astronauts more than outweighs any potential benefits. Cynics argue that NASA's entire Sharks in Space programme is more about selling merchandise than any scientific research. SiS posters, key rings and lunchboxes have been NASA's number one source of non-government revenue since 1986.

Once Bitten, Twice Dead

The lurker shark mates for life. However, as mating always ends with the female biting the male's head off, this isn't a huge commitment.

The not-so-happy
lurker shark couple

Jumping The Shark

While shark-themed nature television shows continue to be popular, there have been several notable flops in recent years when programme makers stray from the factual realm. These include *America's Next Top Shark*, *I'm a Shark, Get Me Out of Here*, *Temptation Shark*, *Sharks in the Attic*, *Judge Shark*, *Dancing with the Sharks* and *Antique Sharkshow*.

A still from Bulgarian TV's
Dancing with the Sharks

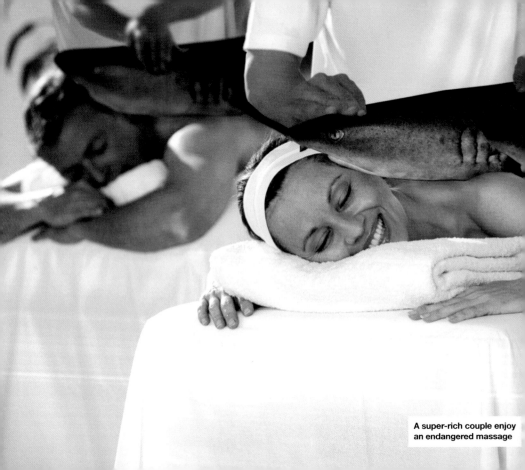

**A super-rich couple enjoy
an endangered massage**

Swanderlust

At $15,000 per session, the most expensive beauty therapy in the world is Dubai's Golden Tree Spa's Sharksfoliation Treatment. Two sedated reef sharks are massaged over the client's naked body to remove dry skin before he or she is blotted dry with polar bear cubs. This is followed by an hour sitting still in a darkened room with a swan.

Protesters outside a Christchurch law court demand the release of the Finding Nemo Three

Sharktistic Merit

Impersonating a shark carries a mandatory 10-year jail sentence in New Zealand. It took lawyers three months to secure the release of three dancers arrested following the opening-night performance of *Finding Nemo On Ice* in Christchurch in 2007. The law has since been changed to specify 'impersonating a shark in or on non-frozen water'.

The Good, The Bad And The Plugly

In the northern hemisphere, a sharkplug is a wax plug that when inserted into the shark's left ear cavity, suppresses its appetite. Potential man-eating sharks living close to major tourist resorts in the Mediterranean are plugged annually in time for the tourist season, and then unplugged after it. Sharks with their sharkplug left in usually starve to death.

In the southern hemisphere, a sharkplug is any shark that has been inflated with air to fill a hole in a boat that has sprung a leak. Sharks used as shark-plugs also usually starve to death.

Professor Sophocles Manasiadis
of the Greek Maritime Institute
performs a de-plugging

Picture Credits and Acknowledgements

All images © Getty Images with additional artwork by Mike Ahern, apart from Fact 13 © David Shen, Seapics.com

Additional shark corralling by the following masters of their craft:
Fact 7 photograph by Lucy O'Doherty; Fact 23 illustration by Enda Loughman; Fact 38 & Fact 71 illustration by Chris Judge; Fact 56 illustration by Mark Wickham; Fact 64 illustration by Ronan McMeel; Fact 81 illustration by Fergal Brennan. The copyright for these illustrations lies with the Authors.

The Authors wish to thank the following:
Rosemary Davidson, Lisa Hannigan, Naomi Derrick, Nick Coyle, Daniel Kitson, Renate Henschke.

In memory of Jasper Legge.